P9-BTY-442

BLAIRSVILLE SENIOR HIGH SCHOOL
BLAIRSVILLE, PENNA

THE HORSE LIBRARY

T 31923
L

THE HORSE LIBRARY

THOROUGHBRED RACING

KENT BAKER

CHELSEA HOUSE PUBLISHERS
PHILADELPHIA

Frontis: Thoroughbreds are bred for racing, steeplechasing, hunting, and show jumping, and they are used to improve other breeds.

CHELSEA HOUSE PUBLISHERS

EDITOR IN CHIEF Sally Cheney
ASSOCIATE EDITOR IN CHIEF Kim Shinners
PRODUCTION MANAGER Pamela Loos
ART DIRECTOR Sara Davis

STAFF FOR *THOROUGHBRED RACING*

EDITOR Sally Cheney
ASSOCIATE ART DIRECTOR Takeshi Takahashi
SERIES DESIGNER Keith Trego

CHESTNUT PRODUCTIONS AND CHOPTANK SYNDICATE, INC.

EDITORIAL AND PICTURE RESEARCH Mary Hull and Norman Macht
LAYOUT AND PRODUCTION Lisa Hochstein

©2002 by Chelsea House Publishers, a subsidiary of Haights Cross Communications. All rights reserved. Printed and bound in the United States of America.

http://www.chelseahouse.com

First Printing

1 3 5 7 9 8 6 4 2

Library of Congress Cataloguing-in-Publication Data Applied For.

Horse Library SET: 0-7910-6650-9
Thoroughbred Racing: 0-7910-6654-1

TABLE OF CONTENTS

1978 Triple Crown winner Affirmed, shown at age 23, lived out his days at Jonabell Farm in Kentucky until his death in 2001.

AFFIRMED

For seven-eighths of a mile Affirmed and his more celebrated rival, Alydar, dueled in a grueling tandem, their nostrils flaring as every ounce of energy drained from their sculpted equine bodies. When they reached the wire in the 1978 Belmont Stakes, Affirmed had frustrated his rival again—this time by a mere nose—to become the eleventh winner of Thoroughbred racing's Triple Crown and stamp himself as one of the sport's genuine all-time champions.

Nearly a quarter century later Affirmed remained the last horse to accomplish this feat. Triple Crown winners are rare because of the stiff competition between top horses, and the demands placed upon the three-year-old contenders, both on and off the track.

"He is one tough hombre," trainer Laz Barrera said of Affirmed during a series in which he beat Alydar by a combined margin of less than two lengths in the Kentucky Derby, the Preakness, and the Belmont. Virtually every time they raced, the more powerfully built Alydar would make a bold move to pull alongside Affirmed, only to be denied victory by the chestnut colt with the heart of a lion.

There was no early indication that Affirmed would develop into one of the Triple Crown's elite members. His pedigree was relatively modest. His sire, Exclusive Native, was well bred (Native Dancer was his grandsire) but had not been overly impressive on the track. It appeared that Affirmed would be a good horse, but not a great one. On the other hand, Alydar was a blueblood from the famous Calumet Farm.

The captivating Affirmed-Alydar rivalry began in their juvenile campaigns, with Affirmed beating first-time starter Alydar in the Youthful Stakes and Alydar getting even in the Great American Stakes when Affirmed carried five pounds more.

Then Barrera took Affirmed to California while Alydar remained in the east. Late in the summer of 1977, Affirmed returned and the two rivals hooked up again in the prestigious Hopeful Stakes. As was to become a trademark of their battles, Affirmed reached back for a little extra and inched ahead as they hit the finish line.

In the Futurity Stakes, Alydar again drew even, but could not pass, and Affirmed won by inches. Alydar then took the Champagne Stakes on a muddy track, so when they tangled for the last time that year in the Laurel Futurity, Alydar was the betting favorite. Affirmed prevailed by a neck.

"He was basically the best horse I ever rode," jockey Steve Cauthen said of Affirmed. "He loved to race."

During the following winter, Affirmed grew stronger and he no longer looked overmatched physically by his rival for the lucrative three-year-old season. Meanwhile, Alydar, who remained in the East while Affirmed again went West,

Affirmed and Steve Cauthen, right, nose ahead of Aydar and Jorge Velasquez to win the 1978 Preakness.

crushed the field in Florida's Flamingo Stakes and the Florida Derby, going $1^1/8$ miles each time in 1:47.5.

Delayed in training by poor weather, Affirmed eventually caught up to Alydar in the Santa Anita Derby, a Kentucky Derby preparatory race, which he won by eight lengths. Both won convincingly in their next starts, setting up the historic first meeting for the Triple Crown in Kentucky. At 6-to-5 odds, Alydar was again a slight betting choice. But Affirmed had a much better ride and was never endangered by the rallying Alydar.

Two weeks later, the Preakness crowd finally gave Affirmed top billing, betting him down to 1-to-2 odds. As usual, Affirmed set the pace in the early stages of the race while Alydar laid back. Coming into the stretch, Alydar launched his move and reached Affirmed's throatlatch. He never overtook him and Affirmed won by a neck.

"I don't know how he keeps doing it," said Alydar's trainer, John Veitch.

Three weeks later, he did it again over $1^1/2$ miles, a distance many experts felt would be too long for him. Veitch believed Alydar could wear down his rival by attacking him earlier in the race, but again he underestimated Affirmed's great resolve. They raced as a team, and Alydar actually poked ahead at one point in the stretch. But Affirmed had

Steve Cauthen

Nicknamed "Stevie Wonder" and "The Million Dollar Man" during Affirmed's Triple Crown pursuit, jockey Steve Cauthen went on to ride 2,794 winners during a career that spanned 1976 through 1993.

After increasing weight and a slump began to bother him in America, Cauthen continued to ride in Europe, where weight allowances are more liberal. He is the only jockey ever to win the Kentucky, Epsom, Irish, French, and Italian Derbies.

A member of the Racing Hall of Fame, he is now associate vice president of Turfway Park in his native Kentucky.

An aerial view of the 1978 Kentucky Derby shows Affirmed, ridden by 18-year-old Steve Cauthen, crossing the finish line just ahead of Alydar.

even more strength, caught up, and shoved his nose in front to make history. Not until the Belmont was secured did Affirmed's doubters fully drop the idea that Alydar was the better horse. They had to reluctantly admit that Affirmed, who had survived the toughest Triple Crown run in history, should be hailed as number one.

It was a fitting conclusion to one of the most storied rivalries ever in horse racing. Late trainer Woody Stephens called the series "the greatest act horse racing has ever seen."

As a four-year-old, Affirmed captured seven straight races, climaxing his career with a victory in the Jockey Gold Cup over Spectacular Bid, who was denied the 1979 Triple Crown by a quirky injury. When he was retired to stud duty after his four-year-old campaign, Affirmed had won 22 races in 29 starts, including 14 Grade I stakes, and he had earned $2,393,818. He was a champion at ages two and three and Horse of the Year at ages three and four. Just once in his career he finished farther back than third.

His offspring have been moderately successful on the track. Like all the best runners, Affirmed has been chastised for not siring one as great as himself. Most of his top off-spring were strongest on the turf. Of his more than 700 foals, 75 were stakes winners.

In January 2001, at age 26, Affirmed was euthanized following a long battle with leg problems. His jockey Steve Cauthen said, "he was basically the best horse I ever rode, the most intelligent. He was just a horse of tremendous courage. He loved to race."

A classic case of rising above his pedigree, Affirmed was proof positive that a lot of heart can go a long way in Thoroughbred racing. He was a magnetic performer.

Not all horses are able to pass their traits on to their offspring, but
Storm Cat is famous for producing big horses like himself. He has
consistently led the North American general and juvenile sire lists
and, by 1999, his offspring had set a record of $10,381,356 in earnings.

BREEDING A RACEHORSE

Horseracing had been a pastime for centuries in many parts of the world before English knights returned from the 11th century Crusades with swift Arab horses that provided the foundation for modern racehorses. Over the next four centuries, an increasing number of hot-blooded Arab stallions were imported and bred to English mares to produce horses that combined speed, endurance, beauty, and the ability to adapt to a variety of climates. This was the genesis of the English Thoroughbred horse, the world's premier breed.

The exact origin of the Thoroughbred is shrouded in controversy because racing was an integral part of English sport for

Secretariat watches the proceedings from the winner's circle after taking the 1973 Kentucky Derby on his way to Triple Crown glory. At that year's Belmont, Secretariat stunned racing fans everywhere with a 31-length victory and a world-record time of 2:24 for 1¹/₂ miles.

centuries before the development of the Thoroughbred in the 17th century. One theory maintains that there was already a well-established breed of native runners before the importing of the Oriental blood. Another theory contends that the Thoroughbred is really the property of both Great Britain and Ireland because of closely linked breeding industries.

King Charles II (1660–1685) rapidly expanded racing by contracting with James D'Arcy, the Master of the Royal Stud, for "twelve extraordinary good colts" annually for the royal stud at Sedbury, in the region that became the cradle of the Thoroughbred horse.

D'Arcy and other breeders went to the Arabian, the most genetically pure breed in the world. Approximately 200 horses of Middle Eastern roots—three-fourths of them stallions, the rest mares—were imported after 1660. About half were Arabians and the rest were closely related breeds from North Africa. Few of them raced; their purpose was to improve genetic lines.

All modern Thoroughbreds descend in the male line from three stallions: the Darley Arabian, the Godolphin Barb, and the Byerley Turk. On the female side, the pervasive influence is the Arabian foundation mare, Old Bald Peg, who was by an unnamed Arabian sire. Hundreds of thousands of her offspring appear in the pedigree of future British runners.

The Darley stud was the founder of the Eclipse line. Eclipse—for whom the annual national Thoroughbred racing awards are named—was unbeaten in 18 starts, including

The Ideal of the Species

The term "Thoroughbred" was not used until 1821 when it appeared in the second volume of *Weatherby's General Stud Book*, which had been established earlier to keep reliable records of pedigrees, matings, and racing performances. After years of crossbreeding with Arab horses, the Thoroughbred finally became a recognized breed of its own.

Thoroughbreds are considered the ideal of the species because of their speed, ease of ride, balance, and symmetry. They far exceed their progenitor, the Arab, in these respects and yet still retain the fire and courage of that hot-blooded breed. The Thoroughbred has, however, lost much of the soundness of the Arab horse through generations of confined breeding and the rush to get them to the racetrack.

eight walkovers, and he sired the winners of 344 races, including three Epsom Derbies. (The Epsom Derby is the English equivalent of a Triple Crown race).

Darley was also responsible for the first great racehorse, Flying Childers (1715), another unbeaten runner and brother to Bartlett's Childers, who never raced but founded an enduring male line as a sire.

Eclipse and his contemporary Herod carried heavy weights over long distances and their races were often run in heats. By the time their grandchildren were competing, youth, short distances, and speed were in style. By 1860, only 16 percent of horses racing in Britain were five years old or more.

British settlers brought horses and racing with them to America. The first racetrack was laid out on Long Island in 1665. The "my horse can beat your horse" mindset of rural farmers, and the inauguration of state and county fairs, prodded interest in the sport, but organized racing did not flourish until after the American Civil War.

With an industrial economy booming, gambling on horse racing grew; by 1890, 314 tracks were operating. Four years later, the American Jockey Club was formed to regulate the sport. By 1908, a mere 25 tracks were left because almost all states had banned bookmaking. But later that year, the introduction of pari-mutuel betting for the Kentucky Derby revitalized the sport as state legislatures agreed to legalize betting in exchange for a share of the money wagered.

After World War I, prosperity reigned and Man o' War—the Babe Ruth of horse racing—arrived, bringing spectators to the tracks in droves. Since then, Thoroughbred racing has had its ups and downs with the last great resurgence occurring in the 1970s with the popularity of Triple Crown winners Secretariat, Seattle Slew, and Affirmed.

One of the most important modern sires was Bull Lea, the first stallion to sire offspring that earned more than $1 million on the track.

The introduction of satellite wagering, whereby patrons at one track can bet on and view races from numerous other sites daily, helped reverse declines in on-track attendance and betting at many facilities.

Breeding Thoroughbreds is an inexact science. The basic theory is that horses with superior racing ability will pass that ability to their progeny, and that certain pedigrees are more likely to pass their racing talent to offspring. There is no failsafe system. Basically, horse owners try to match the best mothers and fathers via a variety of factors: the stud price, racing records of the stallion and mare, their conformation, temperament, soundness, and fertility.

"It's very important to breed like to like," said William Boniface Jr. of Maryland's Bonita Farm. "You don't want a great big mare mating with a small stallion. And if you have a mare with weak feet, you want a stallion with strong ones. What you want is to get more probabilities in your favor."

Sunday Silence, left, went nose to nose with Easy Goer at the 1989 Preakness Stakes, but he emerged the winner. He won 9 of 14 starts in the United States, including the Kentucky Derby and the Breeder's Cup Classic. As of 2000, his offspring had earned over $238 million.

"A lot of breeding has to do with being practical," added Maryland trainer-breeder Richard Small. "The price is a factor. You try to match physical appearances and don't try to breed extremes to get to the middle."

America's first great sire was Lexington, who reigned as this country's leading sire for 14 straight years before dying in 1875. The first notable modern sire was probably Man o' War, whose offspring included 1937 Triple Crown winner War Admiral. Since his owner allowed him to be bred only to the mares of owners of his own choosing, his influence was minimized, but he still appears in pedigrees today, mostly via daughters who became solid broodmares.

In 1947 Bull Lea became the first stallion whose offspring produced more than $1 million in earnings on the track. Bull Lea ruled as number one five times. The $1,630,655 earned by his get in 1952 set a temporary record. In 1987 the descendants of a horse named Mr. Prospector earned $8,986,790. A modest achiever on the track, Mr. Prospector entered stud in 1974 for a fee of $7,500 and became a legend. By 2000, a year after his death, he had generated a record 172 stakes winners.

The price of breeding one horse to another depends on the horses' records. At first the owner of Northern Dancer charged $10,000. One year 10 of his 18 offspring won stakes races. His fee rose to over $1 million.

For breeding purposes, stallions have a higher value than mares because they can mate multiple times annually. The worth of champions, especially Triple Crown winners and big money earners, is so high that breeding syndicates are created in which shares are sold. A single share can cost millions of dollars.

In 1983 Englishman Robert Sangster and Sheikh Maktoum of Dubai, Saudi Arabia, conducted a bidding war at Keeneland for a Northern Dancer colt. The final price was $10,200,000. The record for a yearling later became $13.1 million.

The offspring of a horse named Storm Cat, considered a master at producing big horses, set a record of $10,381,356 in earnings in 1999.

Overseas, North America's 1989 Horse of the Year, Sunday Silence, who stands in Japan, had sired the earners of $238 million through 2000.

From birth, Thoroughbreds are handled extensively by humans to expedite their training and prepare them for the track by age two.

TRAINING A RACEHORSE

Breeding patterns tend to cause most births to occur in the spring; but no matter when a horse is foaled, it is said to be one year old on January 1st of the following year. At approximately five months of age, foals are weaned off their mother and begin a growth period that includes romping with their contemporaries and spending time by themselves.

Thoroughbred horses are natural runners and jumpers, but they must be taught how to accept weight upon their backs, to obey commands, and to respond to urging.

Formal training begins when the Thoroughbred is a yearling. The handler establishes trust with the animal then gradually leads

23

him or her through a progression of steps. This "breaking in" phase usually occurs in the autumn of the yearling year. The horse must learn to be handled, to accept a saddle and bridle, to have a rider on its back, and eventually, to break from a starting gate and run around an oval track.

Owners and trainers try to have their horses prepared for the track by the age of two, when the overwhelming majority of horses begin their racing careers. Some horses, however, may not mature until later or they may develop physical problems, such as bucked shins, which preclude them from competing until they are older.

The handler must be careful to impose discipline without dampening the horse's spirit. "It's hard to make them do anything," said trainer Richard Small, whose most notable charges include Broad Brush and Concern. "The trick is to try to make them want to do it."

"You like to say you teach horses because you don't want to break their spirit," added trainer William Boniface Jr., whose Deputed Testamony won the 1983 Preakness. "You use slow, baby steps and never get impatient. But it's not a wild west, bronco kind of thing. Thoroughbreds are accustomed to being handled so much from birth."

Methods vary, but most trainers start by familiarizing the horse with the bridle and saddle and having him circle the handler on a lunge line, a long flat rope which the handler holds in one hand. The animal is eventually taught to back up and to turn figure eight patterns. This promotes equal muscle development and balance in the horse.

Most horses develop unevenly with stronger muscles on the right side, so it is imperative that the handlers strive for balance in all the formative stages.

The animal learns to respond to voice commands and other aids, such as side reins to correct the head carriage, and the whip, which substitutes for the rider's legs. During this period, the rider lies across the horse's back to introduce the weight that must be carried. This procedure is called "backing."

Once the animal is comfortable with these lessons, the process of galloping begins before winter sets in. Factors such as the weather, date of birth, and type of horse (sprinter or distance runner) will determine when conditioning begins anew. "If they are precocious, you can start them as early as January," said Boniface.

In warmer weather, the process accelerates. Light jogging is normally the order for about a month, followed by breezing (faster workouts) at distances up to a half mile.

After a horse has learned to accept a bit and bridle and wear a saddle on its back, it may be ground driven with the help of long lines passed through the stirrups of the saddle. Eventually, the horse learns to respond to rein commands and to accept a rider on its back.

Once they are mature, horses are introduced to a training track where they begin workouts of light jogging, gradually working up to faster workouts. Trainers like to accustom their horses to running in good weather and bad, on all types of tracks.

"You want them to get used to being on the track," said Small. "And you put them out in all kinds of weather, depending on the owner. It's a long conditioning process and you're never sure you've done enough."

The next step is usually an introduction to the starting gate, either at a race track or a training track on the farm. Walking out of the gate comes first, followed by jogging, then galloping. At some point, the doors are closed to get the animal used to being enclosed temporarily.

When the horse is ready to race, the owner and trainer decide what level of maiden (non-winning) company they will match their two-year-old to, and at what distance. They use conformation, pedigree, and how the animal has trained as guidelines.

The animal is now a lean, mean running machine, capable of speeds of nearly 40 miles per hour with 35 being the average.

A high-priced stakes horse who has great success on the track will usually have a short career. The lucrative side of the business is in the breeding. Strong bloodlines, coupled with the inducement of racing prowess, make the horse much more valuable as a sire or broodmare. Geldings (males who have been surgically castrated) are raced until they are no longer sound or—if they are failing on the flat track—they may be converted into jumpers.

How often horses run depends on their soundness, the financial considerations of their owners, and the availability of proper races for them. While stakes horses are treated with kid gloves and do not run frequently, a lower-priced

A Dangerous Profession

Riding Thoroughbreds in races or even in workouts can be a dangerous profession. Between 1940 and 1999, 141 jockeys died from race-related injuries. The Jockeys' Guild was formed in the first half of the 20th century to pursue better working conditions and safety, including adequate medical care. Now, all tracks have first-aid facilities and an ambulance on the track site. Helmets and flak jackets have become standard equipment for today's jockeys.

claiming horse could compete much more often. These factors—plus the horse's health and weather conditions—determine the intervals between the horse's workouts before and after it races.

Some Thoroughbreds thrive on constant activity; others are best when lightly worked. All need fresh air, exercise, and good feed and care.

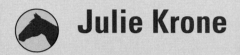

Julie Krone

Only one female jockey, Julie Krone, has ever won a Triple Crown event. Krone captured the 1993 Belmont Stakes aboard 13-to-1 longshot Colonial Affair. Born on July 27, 1962, in Benton Harbor, Michigan, Krone always wanted to be a jockey. She counted Steve Cauthen, the 18-year-old who rode Affirmed to Triple Crown glory in 1978, among her heroes. Smaller than the average jockey, the 4'10" 100-pound Krone took her share of knocks from those in the racing business who didn't think she belonged there. There have not been many female jockeys. Diane Crump became the first woman to ride in a North American pari-mutuel (betting) race in February 1969, and that same year, Barbara Jo Rubin was the first female jockey to win a pari-mutuel race,

In her 18-year career Krone won 3,545 races and more than $81 million in purse money. Krone retired in 1999, having put 17 percent of her mounts in the winner's circle. In 2000 she became the first female jockey elected to the Thoroughbred Racing Hall of Fame.

Exercising horses in morning workouts is the normal starting point for most jockeys, who, pound for pound, are among the strongest athletes in the world. They must have quick reflexes, raw courage, and an understanding of racing strategy and their mount. Usually little more than five feet tall, the bulk of jockeys weigh between 95 and 110 pounds and never more than 117. Before and after a race, they and their equipment are weighed to insure that the horse carried the correct assigned weight while competing. Lead bars carried in saddle cloth pockets make up the difference between the rider's actual weight and the horse's assigned weight.

Jockeys, who wear the patterned shirts and caps that identify ownership of the horse, begin their careers as apprentices, receiving weight allowances from the other riders until they have won a stipulated number of races. Usually after a year, they become veterans, or journeymen.

With as many as 20 horses breaking from the starting at once, the Kentucky Derby is considered the roughest of the three Triple Crown races.

THE RACING CIRCUIT

Of all the racing throughout the world, none generates more interest and prestige than the American Triple Crown. For three-year-old Thoroughbreds, the Triple Crown encompasses the globe's most famous races: the Kentucky Derby at Churchill Downs on the first Saturday in May, followed by the Preakness at Baltimore's Pimlico Race Course two weeks later, then the Belmont Stakes at Belmont Park in New York on the first Saturday in June.

The winner of any one of these legs is guaranteed a profitable career at stud or, in the case of females, as a broodmare. If one horse sweeps all three, the standing fee will skyrocket even

The Kentucky Derby has been run at Churchill Downs in Lexington since 1875. Known as "The Run for the Roses" because the winning horse is festooned with a horseshoe of roses, the Kentucky Derby is always run on the first Saturday in May.

higher. Capturing a Triple Crown is considered the most difficult feat in the sport.

During the last three decades, the Kentucky Derby and the Preakness have evolved into events attended by thousands of revelers who party in the respective infields even though they may never attend any other racing card. All three Triple Crown races are accompanied at their respective tracks by highly lucrative stakes races on the program, and they carry their own purses of at least $1 million.

The Derby is run at $1\,1/4$ miles and is perhaps the toughest of the three to figure because the competitors have been racing in preparatory events in different sections of the country. Furthermore, 20 horses can start in Kentucky, the last six from an auxiliary gate, and it is frequently run roughly, with numerous traffic problems for the jockeys.

At the Preakness, the field is limited to 14. Like the Derby, if the entries exceed the limit, starters are determined by the horses with the highest earnings in graded stakes or in their careers. At $1^3/16$ miles, the Preakness is probably the purest racing test of the three.

Belmont starters are restricted to 16 but, by then, many would-be contenders have been eliminated, and the $1^1/2$-mile test is a deterrent to those horses who are not bred for distance running.

A chestnut colt named Aristides captured the first Kentucky Derby in 1875, and the race has been run annually ever since. The Preakness actually started two years earlier with Survivor winning by 10 lengths, still the largest victory margin in the race. But the Preakness was run in Brooklyn, New York, for 15 years during a period of financial trouble for the Maryland Jockey Club.

The granddaddy of the Triple Crown is the Belmont, which began in 1867 when it was won by a filly named Ruthless. This demanding test has been the undoing of 14

Triple Crown Tradition

Tradition abounds at all three Triple Crown events. The Kentucky Derby is labeled "The Run for the Roses" and the winner is festooned with a garland of roses in the winner's circle. The Preakness has its Black Eyed Susans and the Belmont Stakes has carnations.

Each Triple Crown race has a theme song: "My Old Kentucky Home" at Churchill Downs, "Maryland My Maryland" at Pimlico, and "The Sidewalks of New York" at Belmont Park.

potential Triple Crown champions who had taken the first two legs.

In 1919, Sir Barton—ridden by John Loftus and trained by H.G. Bedwell—became the first horse to sweep all three races. The phrase "Triple Crown" was introduced in 1930 by Charles Hatton of *The Daily Racing Form* while writing about Gallant Fox's victories in the three races. Gallant Fox, who went on to sire Omaha, the 1935 Triple Crown champion, is the only horse ever to produce an offspring who accomplished the feat.

The Breeders' Cup championships were instituted in 1984 to determine annual winners in the following categories: two-year-old fillies, colts, and geldings, older fillies, mares, and older males on the turf, and older horses at six

 Racehorse Rescue

Once they are too old or infirm for the track, less-than-successful racehorses face an uncertain future. If they are not desirable for breeding, they may be sold to slaughterhouses and butchered for their meat, which is turned into dog food or exported for human consumption in Europe and Asia. An estimated 6,000 racehorses are slaughtered each year. The Thoroughbred Retirement Foundation, the nation's largest Thoroughbred rescue organization, buys doomed horses and places them in adoptive homes where they continue to lead active lives as pleasure mounts. With support from the racing industry, the foundation also launched an innovative program in which retired racehorses are placed on prison farms and cared for by minimum-security inmates, who benefit from contact with the animals. To learn more about racehorse rescue, contact: www.trfinc.org

furlongs, a mile, and $1^{1}/4$ miles. The November program, which rotates among the major North American tracks, entailed $13 million in purses during 2000, and culminated with the $4 million Breeders' Cup Classic. At Florida's Gulfstream Park in 1999, wagering on the Breeders' Cup title races soared above $100 million nationwide.

Other major lead-ins to the Triple Crown series include the Florida Derby, Santa Anita Derby, Blue Grass Stakes, and Louisiana Derby.

In addition, there is a prestigious array of races for older horses in North America: the Pacific Classic in California, the Pimlico Special, the Stephen Foster Stakes at Churchill Downs, and the Whitney Stakes at Saratoga in New York.

Breeding normally determines at which level of racing a Thoroughbred will compete, at least initially. Then, early performances on the track will decide for the owner and trainer where the horse belongs on the ladder.

"The most important thing of all is to enter them in events where they're equal to the other horses," said trainer Richard Small. "You try to get them in where they can succeed. And they will tell you if they're better on dirt or grass or certain types of tracks depending on how they do."

"It's important psychologically not to overmatch them," agreed trainer William Boniface Jr.

In addition, there are horses who don't work well in the morning, but excel in a race. "They're known as an afternoon horse," said Boniface. Others work well, but underachieve on the track. They're called "morning glories."

Some horses perform better on off tracks and are known as "mudders." In sloppy going, their chances of winning increase appreciably. Others detest such footing. Some show a preference for running on a grass surface and do not succeed on dirt. Others do not like grass racing and love dirt.

Handicap races—usually for older horses—provide for different weight assignments to be carried by the horse depending on the race record. The entry considered superior carries the highest weight.

In races known as "claiming races," a claiming price is stipulated beforehand and trainers or owners can claim a horse after the race for that amount. In this manner, a shrewd horseman can obtain potentially good horses who have been underestimated by their previous connections.

Stakes races derive their name from the entry fee owners must pay in order to compete in the race. They normally involve horses of the same age and sex, but can become co-ed if an owner or trainer believes a filly or mare is good enough to test the males.

There are occasionally match races in which two horses compete in a head-to-head race, as Seabiscuit and War Admiral did in the 1938 Pimlico Special, and Foolish Pleasure and the filly Ruffian did in the famous race in which Ruffian broke down and was humanely destroyed.

When all the horses but one have been scratched from a race, the no-contest is called a walkover. The most notable recent incident of this type was in the 1980 Woodward Stakes when the competition all shied away from Spectacular Bid.

Depending on the site and the race conditions, the purse is distributed to the first through fourth or fifth finishers in the race, with the winner receiving 60 percent of the total, the runner-up 20 percent, and so forth.

At the highest level, a Thoroughbred who is not retired early for breeding purposes can earn nearly $10 million as Cigar did during his record-setting career. The worst thing for an owner is to have a horse that does not earn a cent, as this means all expenses and no income.

Underestimated by his owners, Charismatic, shown with trainer Wayne Lukas and the late jockey Chris Antley, was once entered in a claiming race. But he and Antley went on to win the first two legs of the Triple Crown in 1999. At the Belmont Stakes, Charismatic exhausted himself trying to win and Antley pulled him up just past the finish line. Charismatic turned out to have a fractured leg and had to be driven off the course in a trailer.

Betting is the lifeblood of Thoroughbred racing. Without it, the sport would shrink dramatically in size, scope and significance. The most common form of wagering is pari-mutuel, a system developed by Frenchman Pierre Oller in the late 19th century. Translated from the French, pari-mutuel means "betting among ourselves." Under this arrangement, bettors bet against each other through a common pool after a percentage of the money is taken out

Track condition affects a horse's performance. Some horses don't run well on a sloppy or "off" track, but those that do, known as mudders, post favorable odds on an off track.

for track expenses, race purses, and state taxes. This take-out varies depending on the type of wager, but is normally between 14 percent (for straight bets like win, place, and show) to 28 percent (for the more exotic bets like the super-fecta). Whatever remains is placed in a pool and divided by the number of wagers on each horse to determine the odds. If a horse is listed at 3-to-1 odds on the track tote board, that means it will pay $3 for every $1 wagered if it wins. The tote board or television monitors are always visible to the patrons and the odds are re-computed at selected intervals until post time when betting on the race is closed.

Types of wagers vary from track to track, but generally bettors can select a horse to finish first, second, or third, select the top two (exacta or perfecta), three (trifecta), or sometimes four (superfecta) finishers in an individual race, choose the winners of two consecutive races (daily double), the first two horses in a race in any order (quiniela) or the winners of three straight events (pick three) or more. The amount wagered can vary from $1 per bet to an unlimited sum. After the race has been declared official by the stewards, patrons may cash winning tickets, either with a live teller or at an automated tote machine.

In today's racing climate, satellite transmissions from numerous other tracks (including overseas) are beamed to the home track for wagering purposes. It is not uncommon for a bettor to have a choice of 30 different tracks on which to bet from noon until midnight. By 1993, simulcasting accounted for 40 percent of all the wagering conducted at American tracks. Telephone betting and internet wagering services have also sprung up within the last decade.

Off-track betting sites in most states which conduct racing allow the bettor to avoid charges associated with attending the races live (parking, admission, etc.) and still wager.

Many horseplayers claim to have a system to beat the game, but there has never been a foolproof one developed. The best idea: get as much information as you can, then rely on your luck.

In 1973 Secretariat
appeared on the covers
of *Time, Newsweek,* and
Sports Illustrated after
he became the first horse
since Citation in 1948 to
win the Triple Crown.

RACING LEGENDS

Eleven Thoroughbreds have withstood the rigors to win the Triple Crown. Others, like Kelso, Forego, and Cigar, gained their fame and fortune as older horses.

More common are horses widely heralded as potential Crown winners, who, ultimately, fail. Recent examples include Arazi, who finished eighth in the 1992 Kentucky Derby, and Fusiachi Pegasus, who won the Derby but was beaten by Red Bullet in the 2000 Preakness on a sloppy track.

Although Sir Barton, who was still a maiden when he entered the 1919 Kentucky Derby, was the first to win the Triple Crown, it was one of his contemporaries, Man o' War, who was hailed

Man o' War, shown in 1941 at age 24, was very close to his longtime groom Will Harbut, above. Harbut always described him as "the mostest horse." Man o' War died just one month after Harbut's own death in 1947.

as the first great Thoroughbred race horse. Man o' War beat Sir Barton easily in a match race at Kenilworth Park in Canada in their only meeting.

The most famous horse never to race in the Kentucky Derby, Man o' War is still remembered as the yardstick by which Thoroughbreds are measured. He raced 21 times, winning 20, and retired as the leading money winner at the time with $249,465 in earnings.

According to a 1997 article by Maryjean Wall in the *Lexington Herald-Leader*, the circumstances surrounding Man o' War's only defeat in the 1919 Sanford Memorial Stakes are cloaked in mystery. Man o' War was "turned sideways at the start" when started by substitute starter Charles H. Pettingill, who was in his 70s and had already made several bad starts in preceding races. With the starting gate not yet invented, horses broke from a webbed tape strung across the track, and Man o' War was known for breaking through the barrier. He broke through five times before the race began.

"Jockey Johnny Loftus was backing up Man o' War, trying to line him up again after the fifth lunge through the tape," wrote Wall. "Without warning, Pettingill sprang the webbing, catching Loftus off guard—and Man o' War facing sideways."

Off to a bad start, Loftus tried to save ground, then get through, but was blocked. He had to swing outside and lost by a half-length to Upset, who was carrying 15 fewer pounds. In five other meetings, Man o' War beat Upset every time.

Another bizarre happening accompanied the match race with Sir Barton. As Man o' War passed the finish line the winner, jockey Clarence Kummer stood up in the stirrups and the right one snapped, nearly causing a fall. At the unsaddling, it was discovered that the stirrup leather had been cut with a sharp instrument although Man o' War had been heavily guarded before the race.

🐎 Worrisome Warrior

A strapping, bold animal who knew no fear while racing, Man o' War had the idiosyncrasy of worrying between races, and he would chew his hooves in his stall.

To ease his anxiety, he was kept company by a fox hunting horse named Major Hunter.

Man o' War set three world records, two American records, and three track records, breaking most of them easily. He carried up to 138 pounds, conceding as many as 30 to many of his opponents, and still won convincingly. The Jockey Club handicapper, Walter S. Vosburgh, intended to put more weight on him than any horse had ever carried as a four-year-old, prompting his owner, Samuel D. Riddle, to retire him after the age of three rather than risk a breakdown. Riddle turned down offers of a million dollars for the horse.

Man o' War's fame has endured the ages. "He was so beautiful that it almost made you cry, and so full of fire that he made you thank your God you could come close to him," said one starter at the 1920 Travers.

If any horse in modern times ever approached the renown and popularity of Man o' War, it was "Big Red," 1973 Triple Crown winner Secretariat. The public was starving for a champion at the time, the Triple Crown having eluded all Thoroughbreds since Citation in 1948. A big, well-muscled chestnut colt with a star on his forehead, Secretariat was the perfect fit. He had an engaging personality and a handsome look that made him the darling of thousands. Twice named Horse of the Year, Secretariat appeared on the covers of *Time*, *Newsweek*, and *Sports Illustrated*.

A son of Bold Ruler out of a Princequillo mare, bred in Virginia, Secretariat was ridden by Canadian jockey Ron Turcotte, who was later paralyzed in a track accident, and trained by Lucien Laurin in New York. His trademark move was on the final turn, a swoosh that powered him beyond all competitors in almost effortless fashion.

Secretariat proved more vulnerable than Man o' War, losing five times during a 21-race career, and he always had

Man o' War was so beloved that when he died of a failing heart at age 30 in 1947, he was embalmed and laid out in a coffin for two days so the public could pay their respects. Thousands attended his funeral in Kentucky and today his grave in the Kentucky Horse Park is marked by a Man o' War statue.

disbelievers who did not think that a son of Bold Ruler was capable of going the distance. He proved them wrong. He nearly went down in his career debut, a rough maiden race at Aqueduct, but rallied for fourth. He won his next two races, then beat highly touted Linda's Chief in the Sanford Stakes at Saratoga to prove he had arrived.

By the end of his two-year-old season, he had banked $456,404 and was named Horse of the Year. In February 1973, Secretariat was syndicated by Claiborne Farm's Seth Hancock, then 24 years old, for a record $6.08 million.

Secretariat ran a dull third in the Wood Memorial after taking two stakes, but was still a 3-to-2 favorite entering the Derby, where he became the first and only horse to run the Kentucky Derby in under two minutes (1:59$\,^2/5$ for 1$^1/4$ miles). Only a malfunctioning timer prevented him from setting a record in the Preakness. Clockers from the *Daily Racing Form* timed his victory over 1$^3/16$ miles in 1:53$\,^2/5$, which would equal the Preakness record. However, the official time was one second slower.

But he saved his best for last and became a legend at the Belmont Stakes. In one of the most stunning races ever, Secretariat—dogged by a speedster named Sham for the six furlongs—won the 1$^1/2$ mile test by an astonishing 31 lengths in 2:24, knocking nearly three seconds off the track record. Sham was injured, finished last, and never raced again.

Racing had found its savior. For the first time since the 1940s racing had a Triple Crown winner.

Secretariat raced six more times, winning four, including the last two on the grass to prove his versatility, and he retired with $1,316,808 in earnings. After being stood at stud, Secretariat—like Affirmed—was never able to reproduce himself.

When complications following laminitis caused his owners to put him down in 1989 at age 19, grieving fans from all over the world sent flowers. An autopsy revealed that Secretariat's heart was almost twice the size of the average horse's, perhaps explaining why he was able to accomplish extraordinary feats on the track.

In the 1940s, racing's first millionaire and the last Triple Crown winner before Secretariat, was Citation. To purists, Citation's feats were perhaps the greatest in history because he won a record 16 consecutive races as a three-year-old, missed another potential peak year at age four with ankle and tendon injuries, and suffered all but two of his 12 losses as an older runner while attempting to break the $1 million barrier, the dying wish of owner Warren Wright in 1950.

During his first two seasons, the horse who represented Calumet Farm at the peak of its power lost just twice and underscored his career by capturing the three 1948 Triple Crown events by a combined 17 lengths.

Citation was a bay son of Bull Lea and Hydroplane II, the dam transported from Europe via the Pacific Ocean in 1941 because of the fear of German U-boats in the Atlantic. Citation was foaled April 11, 1945, and placed in the charge of trainer Jimmy Jones, the son of the legendary Ben Jones.

After a late start as a two-year-old, he won eight of nine before opening the next campaign with two victories over older horses. He had seven straight wins behind him before his jockey, Al Snider, died in the Everglades on a fishing trip.

The Luck of the Draw

Secretariat was acquired under quirky circumstances. Penny Tweedy, then managing Meadow Stable, was honoring a deal the stable's patriarch, Christopher Chenery, had struck with Ogden Phipps years before. Each year Meadow Stable was to send two broodmares to Claiborne Farm to be bred to Phipps' Bold Ruler, with each stable getting one foal each. Every other year, they would flip a coin to determine who would get the first choice of foals, with the other receiving the first the next year.

In 1969, Phipps won and took the Bold Ruler-Somethingroyal foal, a filly named The Bride who failed to hit the board in six career starts. The next year, Meadow Stable got Secretariat.

Thus began the pairing of Citation with the most renowned rider of all time, Eddie Arcaro. Citation and Arcaro won the Derby, then the Preakness. During the four-week break between the Preakness and Belmont, Citation won the the Jersey Derby by 11 lengths. It didn't hinder him at Belmont Park. He won by eight lengths to become Calumet's second Triple Crown winner.

He had $938,630 bankrolled as he reached age six. Citation continued to race in deference to Wright's wishes and finally topped the $1 million mark by earning $100,000 with a victory in the Hollywood Gold Cup. As a stallion, Citation was mildly successful with none of his offspring reaching his heights. He died in 1970 at the age of 25.

Citation, center, with Eddie Arcaro in the saddle, comes up on Coaltown, right, during the 1948 Kentucky Derby.

Five years before Citation, with World War II raging on all fronts, Count Fleet, a son of Derby winner Reigh Count, was preparing for the Kentucky Derby. His owner, John Hertz, did not have a high opinion of his chances. Jockey John Longden talked him into keeping the colt. He had mixed results during his early races, then worked an unheard-of 1:08 ^{1}/5 for six furlongs while prepping for the Futurity Stakes. Clockers were amazed that he could run so fast. But he had left his race in the workout, finishing third. He never lost again.

One week after the Futurity, he whipped a strong field by six lengths in the Champagne Stakes, covering a mile in a Belmont Park record 1:34 ^{4}/5. It was the fastest mile ever run by a juvenile. In the Pimlico Futurity, he avenged a loss to Occupation at the Futurity Stakes and equaled the track record of 1:43 ^{3}/5 for 1^1/16 miles. He won the Walden Stakes by 30 lengths. He was so good he was once assigned a record 132-pound weight as a two-year-old.

Count Fleet did not open his three-year-old campaign until April 9 in New York. He won the Longden Wood Memorial easily, continuing a trend in which he would ease up on the Count near the finish line, so assured he was of victory. In the 1943 Kentucky Derby, slowed in the final furlong by Longden, Count Fleet still won by three lengths at 2-to-5 odds. An even bigger favorite for the Preakness, he won by eight. With a four-week lull before the Belmont, Count Fleet won in 1:36 for the mile over a muddy track at the Withers. The stakes record of 1:35 ^{4}/5 had been established' by Man o' War. He was such an overwhelming favorite, bettors won only five cents for every dollar wagered.

Again at the short odds of a nickel to a dollar, his trainer turned him loose in the Belmont with only two mediocre opponents challenging him. He won by 25 lengths and broke the record set by another Triple Crown elitist, War Admiral, in 1937. It was Count Fleet's final race. He had hind leg injuries and was retired to stud.

Only one colt has ever entered the Triple Crown undefeated and emerged from it undefeated: Seattle Slew in 1977. Slew won three times as a two-year-old, capping it with a romp in the Champagne Stakes in the fastest mile ever run by a juvenile. Slew next showed he was a Triple Crown threat with a convincing victory in the Flamingo Stakes. After cruising in the Wood Memorial, Slew was a 1-to-2 favorite in Kentucky. The start was unnerving. He swerved and collided with another horse and for one of the rare times in his career, Seattle Slew was behind early. But he kept cool and charged into second after a quarter mile. He put away For the Moment after a mile, and jockey Jean Cruget let up at the finish to win by $1^3/4$ lengths.

At the Preakness, Seattle Slew was tested early by Cormorant as they ran a mile in a blistering 1:34 4/5. He drew away in the stretch and (except for Secretariat's unofficial time) ran the second fastest Preakness over $1^3/16$

Famous Jockeys

The jockey Eddie Arcaro, affectionately nicknamed "Banana Nose," was voted the 56th greatest athlete of all time after riding 4,779 winners with a unique combination of strength, intelligence, and rhythm.

Arcaro, together with Bill Shoemaker (8,833 winners) and Laffitt Pincay Jr. (still active) are the most successful American riders of the 20th century.

1977 Triple Crown winner Seattle Slew, shown at age 23, is the only horse to have begun the race for the Triple Crown unbeaten and emerge that way. Also the only Triple Crown winner still living, Slew stands at Three Chimneys Farm in Kentucky.

miles: 1:54 2/4. A muddy track greeted him for the first time at the Belmont, but it didn't matter. He coasted home by four lengths.

Seattle Slew was retired to stud at Three Chimneys Farm with his value estimated at a record $12 million. As of 2001, he was the only Triple Crown winner still living. Cigar was one of his grandchildren.

One who didn't quite capture the Crown in 1979 was Spectacular Bid, labeled the "greatest horse who ever looked through a bridle" by trainer Grover (Buddy) Delp. The steely grey colt was deprived of the Triple by a safety pin. Purchased by Harry and Teresa Meyerhoff for $37,000, the Bid was spectacular from the start, equaling a track record in his second start and winning the Grade I Laurel Futurity in record time at age two.

After reeling off seven straight wins, he finished a mysterious third in the Belmont and Delp said that a safety pin had been found in his hoof the morning of the race. Doubters questioned Delp's assertion, but Bid was given a rest. He lost to the older Affirmed in the Jockey Club Gold Cup before launching a memorable four-year-old season that insured his place in history. He mastered Flying Paster three straight times in the Strub series, setting an American record, and beat him again in the Santa Anita Handicap. He set another track record at Hollywood Park, and the weight assignments kept climbing.

In the Washington Park Stakes at Arlington, Bid went off at 1-to-20 odds. He won by 10 lengths and set another track record. Two races later, Delp balked at the 136 pounds his colt was assigned for the Marlboro Cup and lashed out openly at the New York Racing Association. Bid was scratched. An injury to Marlboro winner Winter's Tale led to his scratch from the Woodward Stakes. When everyone else pulled out, too, Spectacular Bid had a walkover.

Spectacular Bid won all five races in which he carried 130 pounds or more on his back. He took 13 Grade I stakes and equaled or set eight track or American records at seven different tracks. Bid retired with record earnings of $2,781,607 and was syndicated for a record $22 million.

Another horse who barely missed the Triple Crown and an unbeaten career was Native Dancer, the grandfather of Northern Dancer. Beaten only by longshot Dark Star in the 1953 Kentucky Derby, Native Dancer went on to win the Preakness and Belmont that year.

Native Dancer was the first horse to become a television star, easily recognizable on black and white sets of the day. After encountering trouble in the Derby, he lost by a diminishing head. He won the Preakness by a head and the Belmont by a neck, both times over Jamie K. Foot problems began to bother Native Dancer, and he raced only three times at age four before retiring. He carried 137 pounds in a nine-length win in his final race.

On grass, one horse stood as the standard for all: Round Table. He captured 14 of 16 turf races, carried 130 or more pounds in nine of those races, set three American records while carrying 132, and tied a track record. But he was not one-dimensional, winning 29 of 50 on dirt tracks at distances ranging from four furlongs to $1^{5}/8$ miles.

As durable as any horse ever, Round Table started 22 times at age three, racing in every month, and crossed America five times. In one stretch, he campaigned for 15 straight months and won 22 of 27 starts. When he retired he was still sound, the victim of only minor ailments during his entire career.

Overseas, many regard Phar Lap—whose death was surrounded by suspicion—as the greatest horse ever. His

🐎 Sire of Champions

Count Fleet proved a worthy stallion, siring 37 stakes winners and leading the nation's sires in 1951. His progeny included Count Turf, the upset winner of the 1951 Kentucky Derby. This was the first instance of a triple sire in Derby history (Reigh Count-Count Fleet-Count Turf). Count Fleet lived to the age of 33, very old for a Thoroughbred.

racing career in Australia began in 1929 and coincided with the onset of the Great Depression. Businesses failed, people had no money, and they were being evicted from their homes. There was no unemployment compensation. In such gloomy times, Phar Lap shone as a reliable horse on which to bet. He won 37 of 51 starts, including 14 straight, was the Melbourne Cup choice three straight years, and carried astronomical weights.

Born in New Zealand, Phar Lap was purchased for the American equivalent of $336. His American-born owner, David J. Davis, was not impressed because the horse was skinny with warts on his head, so he leased the horse to his trainer, Harry Telford, who agreed to train and feed the horse and retain any prize money he won.

Phar Lap was tended by stable boy Tom Woodcock, and they became inseparable. In 1932, while resting on a ranch in California, Woodcock found the horse in great pain. Phar Lap hemorrhaged and died, stunning Australians and Americans alike. An autopsy found that his stomach and intestines had been inflamed, suggesting poisoning.

Evidence suggested that an insecticide sprayed on the ranch might have been responsible. Another autopsy suggested a "colicky condition," possibly from damp feed. Later, some racing people claimed Woodcock had accidentally killed the horse by giving him a tonic containing arsenic to stimulate his appetite. Although many still believe he was poisoned, the real cause remains a mystery.

Of the Thoroughbreds who achieved their greatest fame after their three-year-old seasons, five stand out: Kelso from the '60s, Forego from the '70s, John Henry from the '80s, and Cigar and Skip Away from the '90s.

Kelso was a scrawny horse with a bad attitude. His owner had him gelded, but he only grew meaner. But, oh, how he could run. Kelso was a slow starter because of his skinny stature, and he missed the Triple Crown. He won eight of nine starts, including the prestigious Jockey Club Gold Cup over older rivals. Kelso was the first three-year-old Horse of the Year who did not win a Triple Crown race.

Kelso became Horse of the Year again at four, five, and at six, an unprecedented accomplishment. Later, he had a memorable series of races against the younger Gun Bow and finally nailed down an incredible fifth straight Horse of the Year crown by beating him in the D.C. International in the fastest $1^1/2$ miles ever recorded in North America (2:23 $^4/5$). In the process, Kelso silenced skeptics who believed he could not win on turf. He won five straight Jockey Club Gold Cups and 62 percent of his 63 starts, retiring as the all-time leading money earner with $1,997,896.

Another gelding warrior, Forego, fell just short of Kelso's earnings while taking over the mantle a decade later. A son of Forli, an undefeated Triple Crown winner in Argentina, Forego did not race at two and was a badly beaten fourth behind Secretariat in the 1973 Kentucky Derby after hitting the rail. He skipped the rest of the Triple Crown.

At four, Forego really got into gear, despite spotting opponents many pounds. He gave highly rated Mr. Prospector five in the Carter Handicap and won, and peaked when his assignment dropped to 124 pounds for the Jockey Club Gold Cup, a weight-for-age race. That victory gained him a Horse of the Year title. Forego was Horse of the Year again at five.

Old John Henry was Cinderella with a nasty temper. He wasn't much to look at, and he was sired by a stallion known primarily for being irascible, Ole Bob Bowers. His dam, Once Double, was also a mediocre horse. John Henry was small and "calf-kneed." He was auctioned at $1,100

Cigar, shown with jockey Jerry Bailey after winning the 1996 Arlington Citation Challenge—his sixteenth straight win—did not hit his stride until he started running on dirt instead of turf.

after smacking his head in his stall at the sale. Handlers feared his aggression—he tore water buckets and feed tubs off the walls and stamped them flat. That earned him his name, after John Henry, the "steel driving man" of folklore.

John Henry was shipped back to the sales where this time, Harold Snowden Jr. paid $2,200 to purchase him. Snowden decided to geld him to make him easier to handle. It helped, but not enough, and John Henry was sold again for $10,000 to a Louisiana group.

New trainer Phil Marino found his talent—briefly—but he was traded back to Snowden for some two-year-olds. Snowden got fed up again and had trouble finding a buyer before Sam Rubin bought him sight unseen over the telephone. John Henry won six of his next 19 races and later won six stakes races in a row. In 1981, John Henry won $1,798,030. He finished with seven Eclipse Awards, two Horse of the Year titles, and $6,597,947 in the bank, a true rags-to-riches tale.

Another latecomer was Cigar. Because of his breeding, he raced on the turf with mixed results during the early portion of his career. It wasn't until he changed surfaces that he became a frightening force. The breakthrough came in October of his four-year-old season when he breezed in an allowance race at Aqueduct, then followed with a seven-length conquest of the respected Devil His Due in the Grade I NYRA Mile. Cigar was lighting up.

At five, he won 10 straight, climaxing it with a commanding performance in the Breeders' Cup Classic at Belmont Park. He overcame a sloppy track, which he had never seen, an outside post, and the rigors of a long campaign to run $1^1/4$ miles in a stakes record 1:59 $^2/5$. The doubters receded.

With 12 victories in a row safely in hand, Cigar returned to racing at age six, courtesy of owner Allen Paulson. In his second race of 1996, he went to the new $5 million Dubai World Cup after missing some training because of a quarter crack in his hoof. Against the world's best horses, the streak could be seriously jeopardized. Another American horse, Soul of the Matter, briefly headed Cigar in the stretch, but Cigar dug in and won at the wire to become a world hero for Paulson, trainer Bill Mott, and jockey Jerry Bailey. Citation's record of 16 straight was in sight.

After a few months off to rest, Cigar went to the Massachusetts Handicap at Suffolk Downs to carry a career-high 130 pounds. It didn't matter. He won comfortably.

The "Arlington Citation Challenge" was contrived for Cigar's shot at tying the record. Dramatic Gold ran a huge

Skip Away, shown ridden by Jerry Bailey at the 1998 Pimlico Special, became Thoroughbred racing's champion older horse for 1997 when he won the 1^1/4-mile Breeder's Cup Classic by six lengths in 1:59.16, the fastest time ever for the race.

race, but Cigar pulled away in the final strides to equal the immortal Citation.

Three starts later, Cigar was beaten by Skip Away, who would mount a serious run at his earnings record, in the Jockey Club Gold Cup. The champion was retired. Cigar lives at the Kentucky Horse Park. He was found to be infertile and cannot sire offspring, the saddest chapter in his life. Cigar earned a record $9,999,813.

Trainer Sonny Hine believed Skip Away deserved the 1997 Horse of the Year title (which went to two-year-old champion Favorite Trick) and had a good case. Hine was determined that "Skippy" would not be denied again. He announced his horse's 1998 schedule and told all comers to apply to run with him. Skip Away skipped away with the title at age five, winning five Grade I stakes, one Grade II, and one Grade III. He had a nine-race winning streak going into the Jockey Club Gold Cup before Gentleman bested him in a speed duel on a sloppy track, and late-running Wagon Limit came on to beat both.

The roan colt was always a threat, but three straight outside posts doomed him in the Triple Crown races after he had captured the Blue Grass Stakes. He kept improving and sealed the three-year-old championship by beating Cigar by a neck in the Jockey Club Gold Cup. At four, Skip Away won only four of 11 races, yet earned more than $4 million and took the Breeders' Cup Classic. He was second five times and third twice.

Now standing at stud in Kentucky, Skip Away lost in his bid to repeat in the Breeders' Cup Classic, then was retired with earnings of $9,616,360. Cigar had been knocked down in their only meeting on the track, but he retained his title at the bank.

While the title of "superhorse" has been conferred upon many young runners, only a chosen few have lived up to the billing. They are racing's legends.

1660s	King Charles II expands racing in England; Arabian horses are imported to begin the development of the modern Thoroughbred
1867	Filly Ruthless wins the first Belmont Stakes
1873	Survivor wins first the Preakness
1875	Aristides wins the first Kentucky Derby
1890s	Racing booms with 314 American tracks operating; pari-mutuel wagering is developed by Frenchman Pierre Oller
1919	Sir Barton becomes the first Triple Crown winner
1930	Gallant Fox wins the Triple Crown
1935	Omaha, a son of Gallant Fox, wins the Triple Crown
1937	War Admiral wins the Triple Crown
1938	Seabiscuit beats War Admiral in a Pimlico Special match race
1941	Whirlaway wins the Triple Crown
1943	Count Fleet wins the Triple Crown
1946	Assault wins the Triple Crown
1948	Citation wins the Triple Crown
1955	The Jockey Hall of Fame is founded at Pimlico
1973	Secretariat wins the Triple Crown, taking the Belmont Stakes by 31 lengths in one of the most sensational performances ever
1977	Seattle Slew enters the Triple Crown undefeated and leaves undefeated
1978	Affirmed becomes the eleventh Triple Crown winner
1993	Julie Krone becomes the first female jockey ever to win a Triple Crown race, taking the Belmont Stakes on Colonial Affair
1996	Cigar retires will all-time record earnings of nearly $10 million
2000	General Express sets a world record of :54 3/5 for five furlongs on the turf at Monmouth Park

GLOSSARY

Allowance race—a race in which weights and eligibility are determined by conditions set by the racing secretary

Apprentice—a jockey, normally young or new, who has not ridden a specified number of winners in a specified time period.

Claiming race—a race in which horses are entered for a specified price and can be claimed after the race for that price

Clocker—a person who times a horse

Closer—a horse who runs best late in a race, coming from behind

Dam—the female parent of a horse

Fast track—the ideal condition for a dirt surface, dry and even

Furlong—one eighth of a mile

Good track—between fast and slow, generally slightly wet

Graded race—the most important races in North America are assigned Grades I, II, or III based on the quality of previous winners and the race's influence on other races

Groom—a person responsible for caring for one or more horses, including the washing, grooming, and feeding

Handicap—a race in which the racing secretary or handicapper assigns weights to be carried by the horses

Length—the distance from a horse's nose to tail, about eight feet

Maiden—a horse who has not yet won a race

Muddy track—deep condition of the track after it is soaked with water

Mutuel clerk—the person at the window who takes bets, also called a teller

Post—the starting point or the horse's position in the starting gate

Post time—the designated time for the start of a race

Progeny—term used to describe the offspring of horses

Racing secretary—official who writes race conditions and assigns weights for handicap races

Route race—a race of a mile or longer

Scratch—a horse taken out of a race

Sloppy track—a track wet on the surface but firm on the bottom

Sprint—a race of less than a mile, generally with only one turn

Stakes—races for which an owner must pay an entry fee to run the horse

Stewards—officials who are responsible for enforcing the rules of racing

Track record—fastest time for a distance at a particular track

Trainer—the person who conditions the horses, is responsible for its well being, and decides when and where the horse will race

Bolus, Jim, and Richard Stone Reeves. *Royal Blood: Fifty Years of Classic Thoroughbreds.* Lexington, Kentucky: Eclipse Press, 1994.

Davidson, Margaret. *Five True Horse Stories.* New York: Scholastic, 1989.

Driscoll, Laura and Margo Lundell. *Horses: An Abridgement of Harold Roth's Big Book of Horses.* New York: G.P. Putnam and Sons, 1997.

Rodenas, Paula, editor. *Random House Book of Horses and Horsemanship.* New York: Random House, 1997.

Savage, Jeff. Julie Krone: *Unstoppable Jockey.* Minneapolis, Minnesota: Lerner, 1996.

Staff of the Blood-Horse. *Thoroughbred Champions: Top 100 Racehorses of the 20th Century.* Lexington, Kentucky: Eclipse Press, 1996.

Stewart, Gail. *The Thoroughbred Horse: Born to Run.* Minnetonka, Minnesota: Capstone Press, 1995.

Twelveponies, Mary. *Starting the Colt: The First Two Years of Your Horse's Life.* Boston: Houghton Mifflin Company, 1992.

page:

2:	Barbara D. Livingston
6:	Barbara D. Livingston
9:	Barbara D. Livingston
10:	Courtesy of Maryland Jockey Club, Laurel Park, and Pimlico Race Courses
12:	© Sames/Livingston Collection
14:	Barbara D. Livingston
16:	Barbara D. Livingston
19:	© Sames/Livingston Collection
20:	Barbara D. Livingston
22:	Barbara D. Livingston
25:	Barbara D. Livingston
26:	Barbara D. Livingston
28:	Barbara D. Livingston
30:	Barbara D. Livingston
32:	Barbara D. Livingston
37:	Barbara D. Livingston
38:	Barbara D. Livingston
40:	Courtesy of Maryland Jockey Club, Laurel Park, and Pimlico Race Courses
42:	© Sames/Livingston Collection
45:	© Sames/Livingston Collection
48:	Associated Press/Wide World Photos
51:	Barbara D. Livingston
56:	Barbara D. Livingston
58:	Barbara D. Livingston

Front Cover Photo: © Barbara D. Livingston

KENT BAKER has enjoyed a long association with Thoroughbred racing, first as executive sports editor of the Hagerstown, Maryland *Herald-Mail,* and for the last 30 years as a sports reporter with the *Baltimore Sun*. He has covered numerous Triple Crown events, including 28 Preaknesses, and still covers daily racing on a part-time basis. He won an award from the Maryland-Delaware Press Association for his photo-story on Barbara Jo Rubin, the first female jockey to win a North American Thoroughbred race. Among his other diverse assignments are collegiate basketball, Naval Academy football, and the Baltimore Orioles' minor-league system. The author lives in Abingdon, Maryland, with his wife Betty.